Alive

Harmeet Kaur

First published in 2020 by

Becomeshakespeare.com

One Point Six Technologies Pvt Ltd.
119-123, 1st Floor, Building J2, B - Wing,
WadalaTruck Terminal, Wadala East, Mumbai,
Maharashtra, India, 400022.
T:+91 8080226699

©

ISBN - 978-93-90543-06-9

Dedicated to

My Grandparents, Sardar Mool Singh Bahri and
Sardarni Diwan Kaur Bahri

Acknowledgement

My third book is an offering to God and my family for being my driving force and keeping me Alive.

Contents

Preface

"I was alive, I am alive, I will be alive if God is by my side."

The title itself depicts the innermost turmoil and the optimistic strategies to be adapted in order to live a demulcent life. There is always an inner force guiding us to do what is right or wrong. We can choose the one our conscious allows. The results will fall in our lap automatically. This third book of poetry, depicts more of my personal experiences with life and how one tries to balance his own self amid these turbulences. This book comprises of three sections.

1. Autobiographical: My interest in writing was lying embedded and I wrote to settle down my emotions. Every single day, I sat in front of God and questioned him whether my wishes would be fulfilled or not. Where there is a will, there is a way. He does things when the right time comes. He gives you the courage and patience to bear the consequences. He can do anything and wants nothing in return.

My life has been an amalgamation of experiences – some harsh and others cool. Being bought up with strict values made life easy and smooth, and these five decades have flown like a bird soaring high in the limitless sky. There are unaccomplished dreams, passions, emotions, likes and dislikes. Never loose heart, because after every sorrowful act there is happiness. My utmost faith in God helped me in walking on the road to success. My strange dreams have come out to be true. I have seen miracles happening and the fulfilment of my dream to become a writer is itself a miracle.

The ones who lose confidence and get depressed easily are losers. Patience is the humblest quality and I have it in abundance. I dream of a literate world because it is difficult to survive with illiterates. My man and my children are my greatest assets. They have stood by me through thick and thin. Embrace all the good things, and keep a safe distance from intolerable people and values. Admire the splendid nature and let loose your senses. Visit the places you wished to. We may or may not be reborn, so why not face all the challenges of this life and have a happy ending.

2.Survival: The Pandemic 2020 has created a ruckus. It is believed that after every hundred years, there comes the pandemic. This annihilating experience sends shivers down my spine and a strange fear has crept in. The virus is deadly. The sudden news of a virus spreading across the world created a lot of disturbance. The normal routine of life was suddenly enraptured by rapid changes at home and workplace.

So many new terms generated like quarantine, isolation, Coronavirus, lockdown, unlock and Covid-19, which has left people confused. The lockdown is a bolt from the blue. Migration of the workers is in process and it has led to untimely deaths. It has left thousands jobless and homeless. The old, young, men, women and children can be seen trailing away loaded with bags and baggage. Their future is uncertain and some breathed their last on this endless path. Thousands have come forward to lend a helping hand to these wayfarers.

It is spreading its roots, and every single soul is standing on a bank, weary and forlorn. The road ahead is vague. There is still no cure and everyone is waiting for D-day. The plan of God is hidden and he wants his people to lead a life free from sins.

3. Believable: The world is a magical place and every single soul is blessed. The essence lies in drinking this elixir to the last drop. We should believe in his presence and creativity. The greatest gift of knowledge marks the difference between animals and human beings. No one can steal this as it lies within you. Try to manipulate the situations you face in life. Don't let your problems create mental instabilities.

We are the saviours sent by God to this world. God created this Universe and human beings for a reason. He doesn't want bloodshed but wants his people to develop cordial relationships.

He wants us to lead a balanced and secure life, free from the impurities provided by nature. The rivers, mountains and the air are losing their immaculacy. The poison is mingling and leaving the people diseased and dying. We have to treat nature as our friend if we want to live an ethical life.

Section 1
Autobiographical

1. My Daily Prayer

O Lord, I fold my hands to speak

Thank you for the world so sweet,

Blessed to be born as your child

Give me the courage to be your Godchild.

Forgive my unmistakable sins if any

Make me do good in plenty,

Thank you for the food and shelter

Make the lives of poor better.

Let love and compassion flow

Let sincerity and equality grow,

I am a crimson rose of your garden

Make me display and spread your fragrance.

2. My Five Decades

The light drizzles on the window pane
That night, my mother was in great pain,
She had maintained her dignity
I was born on 07/07/1970.

My mother was elated
My father was satiated,
They called me their lucky charm
I saved them from all harm.

They gave me a good start
Taught me to listen to my heart
My reading in a convent
Made me more bent.

The values which I imbibed
Have helped me to survive,
In these five decades of my life
My children stand by my side.

God has given me the best

I stand out from the rest

There are hills as well as gorges

We have to bear the consequences.

Don't sit back because you are a woman

You are not less but equal to a man,

Now, at this stage I need stability

I will do things according to my ability.

I want my dreams to be fulfilled

Pleasure and patience to be filled.

3. The Metamorphosis

Whenever I recollect the days bygone

A blend of blissfulness and sorrow made me headstrong,

Life had encumbrances, was never a bed of roses

It had emotions some pathetic, some outdated.

At times, the empty mind gets bloated

In the rivers of trouble, it gets floated,

The roads on four sides are blocked for me

The street that leads to God is open for me.

Whenever I closed my eyes, he was there
He pulled me out from the flooded river,
He gave me the most valuable quality of patience
It has made me capable and humble.

We are solemn, subdued and unknown
We mutate like the larva to a caterpillar,
Then spread and flutter the wings to fly
Like the rainbow coloured butterfly.

This metamorphosis is a gradual transformation
It helps out in making a sturdy formation.

4. A Happy Woman

Earlier, my heart ached
When I was more attached
I longed to be detached.

The thought of being born as a woman
I cursed being born as a human
Now, I stand more competent.

A Happy Woman, more brilliant
I want to open my arms and fly
I don't want to sit and cry.

I'm mesmerized with the vast world
I admire the intellectual.

I am surprised at his creation
The master of all destruction.

He frames our future

The moment I feel his presence,

The time passes

The pain vanishes.

5. Exploitation

Women walk consciously in the open
At their workplace they have chosen,

They hold an equivalent position
Still, they are facing Exploitation,

We are devoted to the work we love
We worship the work for which we thrive,

Our noble work sets standards
We expand the set boundaries,

Even then the complexities arise
You cannot flow with the tides

When a few egoistic men
Break the standards and walls,

She is threatened

She is over-burdened,

She is abused

She is used,

She is considered as the weaker sex

She is not an object,

Slogging for her people day and night

No one is there to see her plight,

Let her work without terror

Do not look up to her for pleasure.

6. Choice of God

God is always a silent listener

He is the mysterious observer

The miraculous and hidden power.

We worship him in the form of idols

We worship him in the form of portraits

His authentic form is settled in our mind.

If we seek him, we may find

All religions impart a similar message

We look up to God for a blessing.

A Gurudwara, Mosque, Church or Temple

Diverts the mankind to a favourable angle

We imbibe the qualities of brotherhood.

26

We try to adapt a decent livelihood

We follow the religion with which we are born

But the choice of God will always be our own.

7. Liberty

Will women get liberty?
I once asked the question to myself

The early years were rough
I was taught that man is rough.

I need to protect myself from hungry eyes
Can I walk alone?

I once asked the question to myself
I was told by the serious and old.

The wolves are loitering around
Will catch the prey when nobody is around

Try to be daring and determined
Allow nobody to come and examine.

To live a secure and organised life
It is safe if I have a partner in life

I was taught by my companions
He will forever be my saviour.

I will walk with him like his shadow
Now, I applaud my liberty

I speak the unspoken
I do the undone,

Finally, I live a life
According to my choice.

8. My Dreams

The day I surrendered to God completely

He made certain things come unlikely,

I started having strange, unbelievable visions

I wake up each morning remembering the scenes.

The bitter truth lies in the fact

My dreams come true, I never falsely act,

Every day, I pray to him before I sleep

So that he sends to me only good dreams.

My dreams are a kind of intuition for me

As they leave me totally in a spree,

They leave me in an inexplicable world

The things will go on and I cannot hold.

I often build houses, huge and beautiful

Snakes often dance in meadows, looking graceful,

I feel horrified at the scene of disease and death

At times, I am drenched in the rain on the heath.

I once saw all the Gods standing across a river

I stood tensed, struggling to cross the river,

They looked and waved at me with both their hands

I somehow reached and bowed myself down at their feet.

9. Do Not Judge Me

I am the master of myself
I live up to my dreams by choice.

All humans are born with a right
To perform tasks which give delight.

I never look up to others for opinions
This will create a standstill to my ambitions.

My weaknesses and strengths
My sentiments and depths

They are mine forever
They belong to me alone.

Do not judge me by your standards
I hold an equal status and degree.

I am capable of balancing in all circumstances
So, dare not create any disturbances.

10. My Language

I spoke one language
When I learnt conversation
My mother tongue.

When I began schooling
I became a bilingual.

Years rolled on
My confidence intact in two
The third followed me.

I now master all three
I am now a trilingual.

What is language?
I now have a genuine answer
It is an art to fathom.

The heart, soul and mind
Through words and sentences.

Some harsh, others soothing

Let the dialogues flow

Like a gentle stream.

Speak, so that others listen

Speak the language of faith

Speak the language of love.

My language

Was, is and always will be

The language of God.

11.The Dark Secrets

The humanity holds close to their heart
Some naked truths of the past,
They will pass on with them
Never disclose but stick to them.

The few dark secrets of your life
It is better to hold on tight,
Let not your tongue speak
Expect the unexpected.

Let your lips be sealed
Let them remain behind closed doors
Never be carried away by emotions,
People are wearing a mask.

Let these black secrets
Never ruin your life.

12. A Friend

Too many cooks spoil the broth

Too many friends buy no mirth.

Stick to one, not many

One who makes you youthful and merry.

She will be with you through thick and thin
Will never leave you sorrowful and grim.

In grade six, I found a friend
From day one, she was awesome.

Her thoughts and tastes matched mine
Her sorrows and joys became mine

On that day, I solemnly declared
She will be the only friend of mine.

We crossed varied phases of life together
From school to college, we grew together.

Marriage made us reach miles apart
We gave life a fresh start.

She knows the reason of my happiness
She deciphers the reason behind my sadness.

My trust in you is taking heights anew
I thank God for giving me a friend like you.

13. My Body

I marvel at myself
From stem to stem,
A skeleton of 206 bones
Blanketed by flesh and skin

Fair, wheatish and dark
Each holds a different façade
I know it is by the will of God.

Every single homework
Is given a different framework,
I awaken to a new morn
I hear, taste, touch and smell

With the functional brain at the pinnacle
I bathe to let the impurities flow
My body holds a distinctive glow.

Everyone possesses a different title

I struggle for my survival,

I live with trepidations plentiful

Have I ever felt my soul?

If never do it now

The power lies within me

Let purity creep in.

On one fine day

When I breathe my last,

My body will turn to dust at last

Only my soul will reach up to God.

14. Penning Down

The volcano of my thought

The lava drifting slowly,

The vent was already there

Then, God wanted me to share.

He handed me a pen in my dream

Made my words flow like a stream,

Still astounded at my talent

He is fulfilling my aspirations at present.

Writing is something magical
Experience brings out things logical,
I had my share of sorrow and mirth
I know there is a reason for me on this Earth.

My writings will make me reach the hearts of people
Let them learn, so that their lives don't crumble,
I write for all ages and coming generations
All individuals have contrasting palpitations.

Writing is fun when I write fearlessly
I delve deep in to my thoughts intensely,
Let me leave my name in this world
Let a few remember me in this Universe.

15. Age Is Just a Number

Our passions never die
Desires touch the sky,
Time never stops for us
Each day is startling for us.

Past moves like floating clouds
Some blue, some grey, others black,
Future stands like a closed bud
It may blossom or remained sealed.

All stages of life may elapse
Let our heart remain intact
We can go footloose and free
No restrictions are laid by God.

You may walk or run at any age
You may play or win at any age,
You may dance or sing at any age
Freedom is to be cherished at any age.

Don't be afraid of the advancing age

Anytime we may reach the winning stage,

Don't be biased be a performer

As age is just a number.

16. The Child Within Me

I am maturing with every new year
I have left in the shade, things so dear,
The chasing behind my school friends
Drenching in the heavy rain.

Sailing paper boats in flowing water
Stealing the fruits from the orchards,
Playing hide and seek with neighbours
Game of stick and stone with friends.

Mischievousness occupied my brain
Certain things I want to do again and again
Gathering marbles in a wooden box
Having the most made me feel on top.

Reading novels in the night lamp
Sprouting with the passing time,
There are friends and no foes
The children have no ego.

The child within me is still playful

It helps me in escaping to a world grateful.

17. Places Don't Matter Hearts Do

I feel uneasy when people declare
A few uncanny, relax and compare,
The world is the most exuberant place
Where every human being holds a special grace.

The birthplace becomes the residing place
We grow up in our own little space,
We travel to distant lands and places
We come across diversified cultures and subjects.

All human beings are God's unique creations
Blessed with a heart full of amalgamated emotions,
There are metropolitan cities, towns and villages
Where people live comfortably of all ages.

There are people good and bad, happy and sad
There are friends and foes, women and men,
Never judge a person by where they reside
Places don't matter, hearts do, so live with pride.

18. The Essence of Smile

What can a smile do?

My reply goes with my experience

A smile can do wonders.

It brings silence after a thunder

It protects you from the plunder.

A radiant smile, anytime

Can make your life sublime.

Greet every human with an amazing smile

Leave your worries for a while.

It can suppress an angry soul

Depressed hearts it can mould.

The essence of a smile is something magical

A gift for all, it is biological.

All enmities come to an end

If smile with a frown you blend.

Create a smiling world for all

Where mankind may come and enthral.

19. My Struggle for Literacy

The notion is not correct

That the average belongs to no sect,

Grasping knowledge and becoming literate

Should be the aim of every considerate.

The gradual steps of gaining education

Reforms the way of the coming generation,

My struggle for literacy began early

I began recognizing the aspects regularly.

Every day I discern something new

I never cease, but I get through,

Every little bit of knowledge I gained

Has given me relief and eased my pain.

Innumerable days and nights I woke up

I compiled my thoughts and became grown up,

The development of my mind became unique

When seriously I took knowledge at its peak.

Learn, attain and maintain knowledge till your last breath

Try to spread knowledge so that you be blessed.

20. My Inspirations

In this journey of life of ours

We come across thousands with a spark,

There are few with prominent grace

Parents and teachers always hold a prominent place.

Since birth, I have heard stories of the chivalrous queen

My first Inspiration is Rani Laxmi Bai of Jhansi,

Her valour, patriotic fervour and sacrifice at such a tender age

She taught women to come out of their cage.

A knowledgeable leader with dream and nobility

My second inspiration is A.P.J Abdul Kalam Azad,

A Scientist and President known for simplicity

He believed that survival is possible if we believe in literacy.

I believe in the preachings of all religions

Each has its own exotic vitality and enthusiasm,

The spirit lies in imbibing them truly

God is omnipotent and needs no identity.

21. Past Present Future

Past is forever following us motionlessly

We wait for a better, new day calmly,

Blended with joys and sorrows were the gone days

We heal ourselves with these experiences.

Present is always accompanying us

We make way for new engagements daily,

We rise and fall from dawn to dusk

Hold on to sincere thoughts patiently.

Future is always undisclosed to us

No one knows who will bear the fuss,

Building marvellous castles in the air

Keep calm and say your daily prayer.

22. Rendezvous

It is a wait of mankind's entire life
This honest truth is always living with us,
That the face of death is horrendous
Till we comprehend it as something magnanimous.

It may come any second or minute
It is the biggest surprise of life,
Every morning, I pray to the Almighty
Let every human being live to the fullest.

If you are blessed with a charmed life
Do worthwhile and stay away from lies,
The kinships we developed while living
Will end in a fraction of a second.

All the things I was holding close to my heart
Will belong to me only till the moment I depart,
There are dear ones who left us late or early
They have made their space in heaven or hell decently.

The queue is long, so stay warm and cosy

The final rendezvous will be nice and rosy.

23. A Teacher

I once asked my teacher when still in school
The rules of becoming a teacher nice and cool,
She guided me in the best possible way
To make good future leaders of tomorrow.

The noblest profession on earth
Requires both seriousness and mirth,
We build every child's future
We want to make his life secure.

We have to maintain our dignity
By teaching them things rightly
Educate them in the best possible way
Let them gain confidence and sincerely portray.

Let us teach them to speak good
Let us make them more charitable,
Let us preach them to love God
Let them get to know the art of love.

For changing them, change yourself

For transforming them, transform yourself.

24. Joys of Motherhood

Marriage makes a woman complete
Still, joys of motherhood is the need,
Two souls are made one on this Earth
A woman is happiest when she gives birth.

For nine months she nurtures the unborn
With the umbilical cord it holds on,
A mother never goes with gender discrimination
For her every child is a blessing.

Sleepless nights and weary days begin
Her life starts crossing varied shades again,
There are sunny days, full of laughter
A smile on her child's lips make her fuller.

She strives to give the best to her child
She can stay hungry to keep him alive,
Her entire life is spent on doting him
My love for my children is unconditional,
I know the pull is gravitational.

25. The Last Breath

I breathe in and then breathe out
The course of life makes me proud.

I crossed the hurdles of life
You stood by me in the strife.

My morning begins with your admiration
Without you there is suffocation.

I gain confidence on seeing you
I love to sit and converse with you.

I need to hold your hand in mine
I know we have very little time.

My eyes become moist when I admit
You are my only love from start to finish.

In these years, I have grown up with you
You made me smile and wiped my tears.

You hold me and there is no fear

When I breathe my last in this Universe.

My soul rises to leave this Earth

Maybe you were the reason for my birth.

You touch my forehead and close my eyes

So that I go for an endless nap in the skies.

26. Escape

I want to escape with you

To a faraway land anew,

Where rivulets flow across grasslands

Where sheep run across the fields.

Where simple men live an ordinary life

Come, let us build a tiny hut,

On the hill top in the meadows

With hay, mud and green grass.

We will live a sincere and fruitful life

Where birds and animals thrive,

Where sunshine peeps through the open spaces

Where dew drops tingle our soft feet.

We will lie down on the lush green grass

Then watch the moon and stars amassed,

Far away from the hustle and bustle

We will have a sound sleep as a couple.

27. Chrysanthemums

My precious
The November flowers,
White, yellow and red in colour
A faint and mysterious odour.

Blooming in my garden
The chrysanthemums,
Growing in bunches
Thin, delicate petals.

Yellow pollens dancing
The Queen of fall flowers,
Some rejoicing the birth
A few lying on the grave.

The mums are gifted on Mother's Day
A symbol of love and longevity
I eagerly wait year long
For the autumn month to come along.

28. The Holy Fair

Millions of worshippers thronging on the shore
To take a holy dip in the river pure.

The ascetics, devotees and saints
Ashes and sandalwood on the body they paint.

In the biting cold month of January
People come from near and far.

I too make my way to the holy fair
The holy cities unfurl themselves.

With tent houses, boats and flowers

I take a bath in the ambrosia.

Vigorous chanting of hymns and prayers

Will refine my body and soul.

The cities enthral the devotees

Displaying an aura of sanctitude.

29. The Golden Temple

It is the holy city of Amritsar
Which I visit with immense pleasure,
The Golden Temple known as Harmandir Sahib
It is the most sacred place of the Sikhs.

In 1577, this abode of God was completed
It holds an auspicious aura of dignity,
The sacred four entrances are open for all
In the middle stands the temple of gold.

Surrounded by a sacred pool
The temple abounds in gems and jewels,
I enter the temple graciously
I bow myself to my Guru patiently.

The circumambulation I take piously
In the immortal nectar I bathe,
My sins are washed away
My soul soothes on listening to the hymns.

The Golden Temple, I even visit in my dreams.

30. Janmashtami

The mesmerising Lord resides in Vrindavan
Lord Krishna, you will be born and reborn.

The day of your birth is an occasion to celebrate
What we can do is to sit and wait.

The clouds still thunder with lightening
The Yamuna is still overflowing.

You will reach your land safely
Your foster parents don't know that you are a deity.

Your land still has your essence
The moment we enter, we feel your presence.

Your magical flute is ecstatic
Your looks are so mysterious
In every form you look marvellous.

Your one look makes the Gopi's and Radha conscious

This Janmashtami, I welcome you again.

Make the world free from pain

In adoration let there be no bargain.

The demons are still loitering

I want to put an end to suffering.

Make this Universe an elated place

I still worship you with the same grace.

31. The Monastery

I once visited a city, fantastic and cold
Up on a hill a monastery of gold.

Five hundred steps I had to climb
For God I could, even if I was blind.

A few broken steps on the slope
We could catch hold of the rope.

Two strenuous hours of climbing uphill

The road to righteousness was full of thrill.

This heavenly sight of the human monastery

All things come to he who waits.

Magnificent with an aura of holiness

A soothing and peculiar calmness.

The stupas and bold architecture

With a colossal Lord Buddha.

The monks were conducting their holy jobs

They sacrifice their life for their Lord.

32. The Night Sky

On a cool, November night

I sit on the terrace, partially bright,

I admire the night sky with my naked eyes

The millions, billions and trillions of stars.

Some outshine while others peep from the clouds

The brilliant Venus, the closest one,

The hues black, silver and white

The sky, moon and the stars aside.

Every day the serene moon in a new shape

Growing from a crescent to a full moon,

It is believed that those who die become stars

I've heard that stars fall on earth.

Maybe the blessed ones come back to earth

The creation of God is magnanimous,

We wait and cherish this sky luminous

To become a star in the sky above.

This velvety look leaves my mind still

The ethereal sky is full of thrill.

33. The Sea Shore

The deep blue waters engulf me often

When I sit on the sea-shore magnificent,

At times, the crystal-clear water gives a shiver

On the silent coast I notice the glitter.

At times, the roaring tides give a fear

See how they come from far to near,

Growing wider and bolder as they approach

Growing higher and higher to encroach.

With a tremendous speed they strike

On the silent margin there is a shriek,

It brings with it joys and sorrows

The tides are wide and sometimes narrow.

Then it starts receding gradually

Pulling all the dirt with sublimity,

Leaving only the wet sand on the shore

Where footsteps leave a mark for sure.

There is no pain only pleasure now

The troubles have vanished from the sea-shore,

The tides have washed away the sins

Now I want to fly with open wings.

34. My Sister in Heaven

You left this beautiful world
Without speaking a word,
God wants only those people in heaven
Those who never did anything absurd.

My sister and companion since birth
I often ask God why she left the earth,
A smiling face with loads of laughter
At least you could have lived for your daughter.

I know you are blessing her from above
She still needs your care and love.

35. This Day Is Last

My eyes open to the sunlit morn
From my casement I watch the climbing fern,
Will it be my last day on earth today?
I silently fold my hands and pray.

If we finally come with such a conclusion
That our life on earth is God's decision,
Every day will be a new one
It is better to be merry than to moan.

Take a pledge to do one noble work
Be charitable to remove hunger and thirst,
Leave all the grudges of the past
Perform as if this day is last.

Gently touch the things you admire
Engulf yourself in the deeds you desire,
Try to remember him night and day
Praise him as he stands unflawed everyday

36. Let Me Touch Now

There are multiple things I want to touch
So, let me touch the things untouched.

The petals of the gigantic flowers
The soft silk thread of the cocoon,
The dewdrops of the lush green grass
The furry coat of a Siamese cat.

The rough bark of the holy trees
The ice-cold water of the melting glacier,
The timid leaves of the touch-me-not plant
The feathery snowflakes falling from the sky.

Let me touch the forehead of my children
I want to give them blessings plenty,
Let me firmly hold the hands of my soulmate
I want to gently hold my mother and satiate.

Let me touch the walls of the temples

Then feel the essence of his presence transcendental,

I want to dress my Lord in dazzling attire with jewels galore

This is the final and most exceptional touch I ask for.

37. Let Me Live Now

Let me live now.

One by one with the passing years, I have grown

By the will of God, I have survived,

A few of them pushed me down to hell

But the strength within me made me stand upright.

Let me live now.

Being a woman my heart overflows with love

It is overloaded with responsibilities innumerable,

My performance is always immaculate

Any given task comes out beyond comparison.

Let me live now.

I have burned several lamps and candles

Made my mind a storehouse of knowledge,

Now I know my pen will never stop

God never wants me to put a full stop.

Let me live now.

As a daughter, mother and wife

I executed my duties with strife,

I was pleasing, pleasing and pleasing

Now my mind is in a more balanced position.

38. Let Me Breathe Now

Let me breathe now.

The fresh morning fragrance of the meadows

The rainbow coloured flowers dancing with the leaves.

My nostrils swell up with the incense

Of the ripe fruits hanging in the orchards.

The raindrops falling on the sand

Its odour travels up to my brain.

At several places the air is venomous now

It makes the inhaling arduous now.

Let us purify the impure air

Let the world get a breath of pure air.

39. Let Me Love Now

The seeds of adoration and abhorrence are sown
In our hearts at times known and unknown,
We come across the singles and multitudes
They are placed like latitudes and longitudes.

Every living thing is God's creation
He never despises but gives adoration,
The cruel, jealous and faithless
The benevolent, generous and faithful.

When the search for loved ones was established
The fake and faulty ones automatically perished,
Few with a dilly dally and mysterious look
The loved ones I could count on my fingers ten.

Now with my choices of love limited
I want to pour on them love unlimited,
They are my weakness and my strength
My fondness will never fade at any length.

40. Let Me Love My Country

In this universe and spectacular space
My country holds a small place,
The traditions hold an aura replete
With customs and mannerisms complete.

The Golden Bird with flying colours
The land of sages and hermits scintillating,
The sun-tanned beauties meditating
The place for Gods and Goddesses to galore.

Where four seasons give comfort therefore
I may have visited hundreds of countries,
Modern cultures are thriving at places
My roots are embedded in my country.

No other place can captivate me ever
Let me love my country forever.

41. Let Me Speak Now

I am no more tarnished
The phobia has vanished,
Think before you speak
Look before you leap.

Will I speak the words unspoken?
Let me speak now.

Countless thoughts occupied my mind
Making my life more sublime,
I am famished and straight
No longer can I wait.

Let me alter my state
The words are stuck on my tongue,
I no longer want to run
Let me open up and not pretend.

Let me now put an end

To the bleak silent past,

Let the heart and soul rejoice

Speak the unspoken words by choice.

42. Let Me Hear Now

I am often driven by a variety of sounds

Streaming in from the air and the ground,

We are the blessed ones as we can listen

So, let us not put a deaf ear to every composition.

The chuckling sound of the baby in a mother's arms

The giggling of children playing in the park,

The gentle laughter of couples in secret conversation

The boisterous snickering of blossoming girls.

The pitter patter of rain drops on my roof

The roaring thunder on a dark evening,

The babbling sound of the rivers

The creaking of the pebbles on the sea-shore.

The chirping of birds on a breezy morning

The cock-crowing in a far-off land,

The mewing of a cat sitting on a wall

The hymns and chanting in the name of God.

43. In Love

I was unaware of a relationship
Until I gained your companionship,
I didn't know the definition of love
Till the day for you my heart did move.

I could never express myself to anybody
But I opened my thoughts to my buddy,
You perceive me to the deepest core of my heart
You wipe my tears to give a fresh start.

You helped me to climb the steps to success
You stand by me at times of distress,
You graced me only with blissfulness
I can survive with you in all circumstances.

My emotions will overflow for you forever
We are always compatible together,
The tasks are now easy, that were tough
It is a marvellous feeling to be in love.

44. Alive

Adapting myself to the realities of life

Learning to dissolve with them by being patient

Ignoring all the negativity around

Voracious reader to a solemn writer

Enjoying every moment with improved fecundity.

45. Puppet

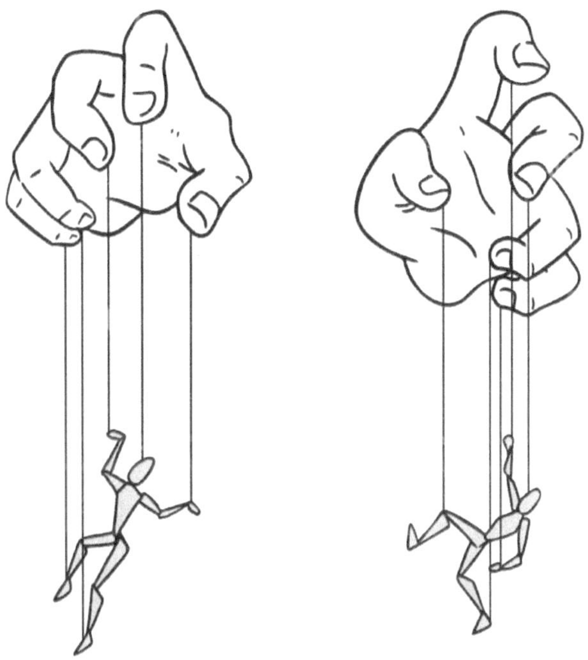

A string is always tied on my head

Which pushes and pulls me with the thread.

I often take my steps by choice

It pulls me if I go for vice.

For virtues it leaves me free

I try to give my finest performance on stage

The audience I always engage.

I twist and turn my hands and feet

The string never lets me face defeat.

I go round in a swirling motion

The freedom lifts me from my emotions.

I always want my presentation to be noteworthy

I know God holds the cord to make my life worthy.

46. A Woman of Substance

Silently, I observe myself attaining contentment
Live life, no need to be repentant,
Time heals the most unpleasant scars
Success will follow if destined.

May there be no bars to confine
Amid these series of restrictions,
I regretted being born as a woman
I now swirl in the garden of wisdom.

I realize, I am the gifted child of the superpower
The holiness I imbibe, drench in the heavenly nectar,
Riches do not fascinate me anymore
Materialistic people hold no vitality for sure.

My stay on this planet is a brief one
Depends, if we go for morality or misdeeds,
The world welcomes and sends us back empty handed
Human beings still hold an ego without any advantage.

Make the most of life, we are born only once

Be a good Samaritan in your last chance,

Admire the stupendous gifts of nature

I acknowledge, I am God's most admirable creature.

I patiently give ear to every critic

I consider myself a staunch feminist,

In matters if I disagreed, I now agree

A woman of substance, I am proud to be.

47. The Art of Patience

My quality to listen meticulously
Makes me excellent and patient,
It makes me survive gracefully
I feel flabbergasted.

When I watch people
Making a mountain out of a molehill,
Abusing and misusing others
Adding fuel to the fire.

The Art of Patience
Is an exceptional quality,
It relaxes the sinews
It brings tranquillity.

Creates an aura of serenity
My priceless possession
I fondly live with passion.

48. If the World Went Mute

Humanity needs to be restyled
Some sit and groan,
The honking of the horn
The airspace going wild.

Gossiping females
Blabbering males,
Commotion at every place
Ears have grown weary.

What if the World went mute?
It will be heaven on Earth,
Silence is grounded at places
In the vast deserts and mountains.

I will fascinate humans
Conversing in symbols,
The tight lips displaying their beauty
Only the sincere voices.

The sound of nature

Will pacify the ears

I will be attuned to God's ears.

49. Someday, Somewhere, Someone

A short and mysterious journey
I walk up to the banks.

Admire the shore in moonlight
The tides will continue to roar
Striking against the rocks on the shore

The earth will do the daily chores.
Sun, Moon and Stars will shine

The living won't be living,
One fine day, they will be dying
Then the doomsday.

Mind will have a gap
Body will be trapped,
Heart about to shrink
Don't be fearful.

Give an expression of cheerfulness

Someday, Somewhere, Someone,

Will travel from distant lands

Make an exuberant appearance.

With divinity at its peak

I will rise from the sleep

The doors will open on its own

I will walk to the path of heaven alone.

50. Autobiographical

Accustomed I am to this world now

Underestimating me there are few

Towards a higher goal I aim

Optimism is brimming within me

Biologically I am a female

Invoking a spark in the males

Overflowing with zeal

Grounded with values I am

Rational and outrageous

Appealing to many

Philosophy is settled in me

Headstrong I go alone

Irritability is not in my blood

Catharsis I follow

Ambivalent I get at times

Lastly, I am a feminist.

51. Rebirth

As a human I am born

After eighty-four lakh births,

My previous one is hidden

I don't remember if I was a cat or a bird.

My behavioural pattern remains the same

I have a fancy that I cherish of and on.

I hadn't harmed anybody

I hadn't committed sin,

I hadn't spoken ill

I hadn't broken a heart.

The life cycle moves on

If a choice was given by God,

If it was a rebirth for me

I would want to be reborn as a Peacock.

The colourful feathers I will display

I want to dance around and play,

There will be no worries only joys

I will climb trees and houses

People will cherish on seeing my tail with eyes

My feathers will adorn the crown of my Lord,

Don't kill me, let me die naturally

Let me live in this birth peacefully.

52. I Am Alive

You pulled me out
From the dark cave.

Full of innumerable rocks
A stream of water flowing,
My eyes started blinking
On seeing the sunrise.

The pleasure of being in the light
Will I appreciate the gifts of God?
The meadows I admire,

Your creation is splendid.

This is the time
This is the place
This is the moment
We will never return.

Feel the pleasure and the agony

Each living thing has a soul,

In the holy Ganga, I take a dip

You hold me with a tight grip.

I swim across and survive

I am fortunate, I am alive.

53. Surrender

The greatest possession in life
Is the way you let go your strife.

One fine day, I realised
Whom to look up to,
In times of distress
When there is no progress.

I looked vacant and worried
I was blank and emptied
The track was right or wrong
I closed my eyes and meditated.

A light shone near my forehead
I was influenced by the gleam
It would have made me blind
I couldn't have seen with naked eyes.

He held my hand, I walked

As if going to a far-off land.

I opened my eyes

A strange vacuum with a golden silence.

I bowed and touched the ground

My door was wide open,

From that day onwards

I believe in complete surrender.

54. Travel

Before I leave for the final farewell
There are mysterious places I want to travel.

This wonderland, built by God
Has numerous, incredible places.

Far off lands, I want to explore and reach
Tranquilize myself with a sun bath at the beach.

I want to sit near the shimmery ocean at night
Watch the shadowy stars twinkling in water.

The seven wonders I want to look at

The spectacular architecture mankind has brought.

A visit to the villages is a must

I want to imbibe the simplicity and the dust.

The thickness of the dense forest attracts me

The animals wandering, give a sense of liberty.

These visits will ease me of my problems

Travelling soothes my soul and leaves me awesome.

55. My Sketches

My sketches of God
Adorn my walls,
He moves my hand
To paint himself
Alone I am nothing
With him, I am everything,
The day I started drawing you
I was out of the blue
I gained insight
I was awestruck,
Your image was settled
In my mind it battled
I began to portray
On a blank canvas,
On white with black
I entered a queer world.

One by one
I sketched all the Gods,
They hold a distinctive place
On my wall, in my heart.

56. Who Will Survive?

Darwin's theory still holds vitality
"Survival of the fittest" has its magnanimity,
With new developing minds and bodies
The scientific and advanced theories.

A new conundrum has aroused
Who will survive?
The comparisons are made
The new implementation carries on.

I blend it with my opinions
I try to gain the majority
Survival in this century
Is possible only through literacy.

Let the new establishments continue
Let us be considerate
The new theory will gain vitality
Let us follow "Survival of the literate".

57. Number Seven

I am not convinced with numerology

It is not my cup of tea,

At certain troublesome times

My thoughts get engaged.

The symphony of numbers

The lucky seven charm,

Maybe it a secret blessing

It has followed me since birth.

My name bears seven alphabets

My birth date has triple seven

I got married and entered block seven

My fingers cease to move after seven

My house number is sixteen

Which becomes 1+6=7,

The number game will continue

Till in this world I discontinue.

58. Humour

Laughter is the best medicine
It wards off the suffering

I laugh aloud and breathe
I feel I am complete

Learn to laugh at yourself
Don't create a laughing stock

Humour is the gift of God
Crying builds up the burden

Laughter lightens up my temptations
I want to create a world of laughter

Where patience will grow
No one will bother

Let there be loads of laughter
Take a break, make yourself lighter.

59. My Dad in Heaven

You made me walk my first steps

I sat on your lap and hugged you tight,

You taught me the art of struggle

Save money to buy a morsel

You worked your fingers to the bone

On stormy days you will be left isolated

You enlightened my future though

Daddy you told me so

You loved to see me smile

You hated tears in my eyes,

A fortunate family on the go

Your untimely death gave sorrow

Your space lies deserted

Your belongings are there no more

No one can fill this void

I long to sit by your side

Your dwelling carries your essence

I can still feel your presence,

You were doing all the things plausible

I know that now my dad is in heaven.

60. My Success Story

I have now written my success story
Since the day I learnt that nothing is worthy.

I have now grown up with the vicissitudes of life
I have learnt that it is useless indulging in squabbles

I have learnt not to mess up with illiterates
I have learnt to give my ear to the appropriates.

I have learnt to fight for my dignity
I have learnt to pass my life eating right.

I have learnt that life is uncertain, so be prepared
I have learnt to stay quiet in front of imbeciles

I have learnt to care for those who care for me
I have learnt to forget the ones who forget me

I have learnt that we develop temporary relationships in this Universe

I have learnt that our soul leaves our body and enters another world.

61. My Village-Dera Bassi

The palatial house in the middle

My grandparents lived there, soft and subtle,

Every summer I reached there

With my village I had an affair

The narrow vilanes and flashy shops

The vendors shouting on top,

The jutis, parandis and turbans

The Patiala salwars and phulkari dupattas

The chilled, marble stoppered bottles of soda

The sarson saag and makki ki roti,

A glimpse of Amritsari munda and sincerity

My farm house I often visited

Where buffaloes and cows grazed in the meadows

Milk and butter flowed in abundance,

I drenched myself in the tube well water

I devoured the food cooked on the brick stove.

Now, there are neither my grandparents nor that house

I visit Dera Bassi whenever I cross,

I stand blank faced outside the house

Tears stream down as I have now lost that house.

Jutis- Moccasin

parandis- A decoration for a braid tassel

salwars-Pleated trousers worn by women from South Asia

saarson saag- Mustard greens dish

Makki roti- Flat Punjabi bread made from corn meal

munda-boy (In Punjabi language of India)

62.1984

I remember the crack of doom in October
There were thousands who didn't see November,
The innocent men, women and children of a free state
Sacrificed in the gluttonous hands of fate

The memories of this bloodshed never fade
I can feel blood trickling down my face,
Some going helter-skelter and others set ablaze
Their hair chopped off, which was their grace

Establishments and outlets were set on fire
Their shrieks reached up to the skies,
A mother was seen holding her son tight
The hooligans pulled him and burned without fright

The families were held captive by them
They were all together put to fire then,
Were they the sinners who were killed?
They didn't even know the reason to be spilled

The dwellings were looted by the rioters

They were chased and slaughtered by the fighters,

The flaming streets and the blazing dead

I never wanted this to spread

I want the humans to have humanitarian values

Let us stop homicide in the name of religion,

Let politics not be amalgamated with worship

Let us create a peaceful world to dwell in.

63. Making My Way

No one can pull me down
I am making my way.

My talent was spreading its roots
I had full faith, in his existence
He was making me feel his presence
My prayers were answered

I was noting down in tit-bits
It had to be compiled,
My inner urge made me
Go with the flow

The doors are wide open now
I am adapting the genres,
Prose, Poetry, Drama and Fiction
I am not waiting for a reaction.

64.The Stroke

My body temperature was rising
I couldn't hear my snoring,
I went into deep slumber
I was not responding

When I was shaken
I thought I was dreaming,
Splashing water on my face
They made me smell the onion

I shuddered and sat up
Wearied look and drooping face
Surrounded by my loved ones
They wanted me to converse,
Words got stuck
I managed somehow.

I was rushed for first aid
The conclusion came out
It was a brain stroke

My days passed in silence

My nights in oblivion,

After several days

For a change, I changed.

I needed mental stability

I needed tranquillity,

I came out more quick-witted

Some new habits I generated,

I now stand elated.

65. Reflection

In you I perceive
My reflection

You are a chip off the old block
Your profound thoughts match mine,
Your style is quite similar
God fearing and generous

You have watched my every step
Since you took your first step,
You appreciate literacy
You despise lies and liars

Charitable and compassionate you are
The apple doesn't fall far from the tree,
Your attire and looks match mine
My precious daughter, you are a reflection of mine.

66. Salute

I salute the soldiers and bow my head

Wrapped in the tri-coloured flag you lie dead

Your coffin is surrounded by the ones you loved

Flowers and wreaths cover your casket

Your mother, teary eyed, peeps through the glass lid
Sees your face all stained with blood.
Your wife and children stand and salute you
For all the daring steps in the war you took

Few among millions die for their country
They are the ones who create history.
You stood alert and armed, night and day
Patriotism runs in your blood upright

You are born for your land
You live for your land
You die for your land
You are indeed a hero, man.

67. Lost and Found

I was lost

In the dreary desert,

Making both ends meet

From dawn to dusk

The daily chores

Killing my desires,

My limited surroundings

My thoughts making a pyramid

Like a mummy I lay inside

Embalmed, incensed

In the dark cave I, a ghost

Then a ray of sunshine

I found myself,

I wriggle out

I throw the multiple garbs

Creeping, crawling out

As slow as molasses,

The suffocation ending

Standing on the mountain top

I inhale and exhale

It's a renaissance

I am lost and found.

68. The Dark Waters

Save them…. save them… they are dying.

The mountains look majestic from where they flow
The snow-white glaciers melt into ice cold streams,
They carry with them the soil and the trees
Voluptuous and meandering among the hills

Reaching the plains with a gushing flow
The translucent waters turning opaque,
The crystal clear being blended with dirt
The sacred waters reaching the shores

From turquoise and deep to a spray of soot
The dark waters reaching millions of dwellings,
Spreading diseases and causing infections
Save the human lives that are priceless,
Make the water free from impurities and pious.

69. Hiatus

The need of life

Is a hiatus,

Take a short break

Have coffee with cake

Climb up the hills

Go for the thrills,

Wear your favourite dress

Play a game of chess

Go to the theatre

Paint a beautiful picture,

Go for horse riding

On the solid ice go for skiing

Smell the fresh jasmine

Drink water with lime,

So many options in life

Can remove your strife

So, cherish your life.

70. Harmeet

He is creating a unique path for me

Arrangements being done in plenty

Rivers of wisdom flow within me

Miracles keep happening of and on

Extending a note of gratitude to my Lord

Empathetic you have made me

Thank you for the unlimited gifts you bestowed on me

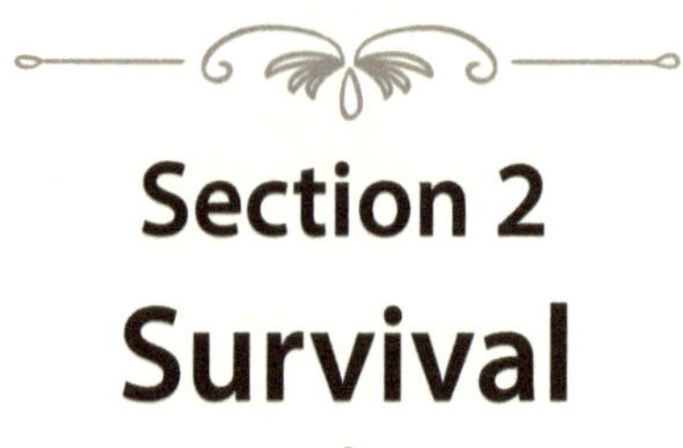

Section 2
Survival

71. The Virus 2020

From distant lands it has travelled

The invisible, unseen symbol of death,

Slowly creeping into the bodies from nowhere

Killing and suffocating humans at large

After every hundred years

Unbearable becomes the weight of Earth,

Few young, old, men, women and children

Will exit this world without a crime

Every single minute there is fear

No one knows when it will be near,

With its countless hands spreading everywhere

Leave the innocent and spare the world

Your sins have multiplied with the growing years

God is calculating since months and years,

Transform yourself and be noble

Spread generosity and be honourable.

72. The Inner Self

Will you spare us if we wear a mask?
The fearful people ask at last,
The mask will make you short of breath
It will hide your inner self.

The choked throat suffers
The face looks austere,
The virus is air borne now
We are not free from virus.

Living in enclosures
Glancing through windows,
Maybe, we are spared
Maybe, we stay alive.

73. The Pandemic

The Pandemic will only end

When the people on this Earth will mend,

We have noticed in the past century

Your sins have created history

Your business is to be egoistic

With your negativity you make others sick,

Learn to love and to bend

Learn to be charitable and to spend

Time is passing at a snail's pace

People are left with a gloomy face

God is in heaven, watching you

He wants virtues to blend with you.

74. Merciful

Mankind is experiencing a tremor

Existing everywhere

Resting and again attacking

Can you be merciful?

Intermixing and interchanging shapes

Fighting to survive on this planet

Unexpected results you give

Laboratories still unable to detect

75. Migration

The streets thronged
Countless, homeless people,
Barefooted and overburdened
With meagre belongings

Quiet, worn out faces
Sweat trickling down their faces,
Engulfed by thirst and hunger
Toddlers holding the little finger

Some sitting on the shoulders

With the sun on top,

Not a single place to stop

A few shady trees

The burning hands and feet

The virus made them leave,

For their residences, they grieve

The migrants meet

From distinctive lands

Holding hand in hand,

The gloomy night appears

The fear lying within

Will there be a new morning?

The pressure builds on.

76. Recession

Slogging day and night
Making both ends meet,
The virus from nowhere
Enters the hemisphere.

Lives tumbling down
No more steps to climb,
Life is still, like a statue
The mind devoid of thoughts.

Few stuck inside their dwelling
Some thrown out in the open,
The doors are shut
People are uprooted.

Vacant, they stand on the road
Not a single penny to spend,
Time is passing without hope
Not a single ray of sunshine.

It may take years to get back

The recession will only subtract.

77. Falling Dead

The graveyards are overloaded

The Earth has no space for the dead,

Dying they are in great numbers

The virus is hitting hard these successors

Trying to run away and hide

In the most secret place aside,

You are visible to the virus even in the dark

It easily makes its way for an attack

The lethargic and warm human body

Eagerly awaits the end of the body,

The masses will not accompany the dead

Take precautions so that it doesn't spread

The streets are lying deserted

We can see many falling dead.

78. Lock to Unlock

The world is locked
Snoring within closed doors
Peeping through the windows
Scarcity of necessities
Absurd livelihood now,
The humanity tensed
Some losing patience

Four walls like prison cells
The depression building slowly
The chanting of hymns
A display of talents
The virus taking a separate track

From lock to unlock

The gradual unlocking
Some going fast, some slow,
Some fearless, some fearful
Everything at a slow pace

The dilemma lying in the mind

To begin from scratch

The things don't match.

Many have lost hope

They find no scope,

The sick and the diseased

Still fighting for survival,

We only need God's approval.

79. Open the Doors

I'm stuffed, suffocated
Let me open the doors now,

These prison walls are killing me
The temple doors are closed
God is examining his people
He was always humble.

He was giving chances
He wanted them to master
The theory of benevolence
You changed your track.

You mastered callousness
Still, people are not afraid
He will open the doors
He too wants to answer the prayers.

Of those who were looking

Through the glass doors,

Wondering, waiting

For the doors to open.

80. Survival

Secretly it places itself on the living

Ubiquitous and deadly

Rampant without ceasing

Villainous it brings distress

Invincible conquering others' lives

Virus spare us

Abysmal for every human

Listen to our prayers Lord

Section 3
Believable

81. The New World

We are towards the making of a new world
Where passions and jubilations will unfold.

There will be no space for enmity
Each individual will have his own identity.

The animals and birds will be saved
The air will be full of oxygen, without any toxins.

The scientists will discover a new vaccine
So that all humans are free of reactions.

We will have all the facilities at our doorstep
No one will punish us; we will be our own judge.

82.War

The dead are lying in the open nameless
The ones who have slayed them are shameless.

The world is at war without any reason
No one knows who is guilty of treason.

The warships, aircrafts, mortars and artillery
The soldiers sacrificing themselves for their country.

The fight may not hold a proper logic
The countries make a show of being barbaric.

The endless fight lives for centuries

Shun the war and stop the miseries.

83. Belief

No need to live your journey with a false belief

One fine day, the path will automatically become rough

We believe that we are distinguished, we can bluff.

That we can live with our sins and breathe

They are being calculated at every step

Give some space to authentic, true beliefs.

That the good live with meagre needs

Have faith in the maker at large

We will be penalized in this birth at last.

84. Magic of Life

Every new day is a blessing for us
We can make our day or go astray,
The blissful days will surely come in
If we set standards and let virtues set in.

The magic of life will anyhow begin
Stay calm, do not let your emotions swing,
God has something special for you
Maybe you are the blessed one too.

85. Nature

We admire and use nature to the fullest

Let us always greet it and consider it sacred,

We should never play with it to see the result

It will be the winner and leave you in distress.

These hills and valleys speak to us

That heights and depths are unknown to us,

Destiny is silently creeping since the dark

Let us be thankful from the bottom of our heart.

86. Rainbow

The vibrant colours of a rainbow leave a message
That after every great loss, there is success.

Build up courage and give a fresh start
Heal up your wounds and do not be hurt.

These seven colours look mystical in the sky
It gives a magical influence and looks fabulous.

Let our lives be full of gaiety and pleasure
Let these hues remove our agony and sorrow.

87. Depression

The most dreadful and painful part of life
When the mind is weary of piling the thoughts
Someone intimate is needed to draw out the undisclosed
It may give a relief and leave you composed.

Lend your ears to the ones lying still
Make way for them so that they don't spill
Wipe their tears and make them laugh
Maybe, they have a shocking past.

Let the bygones be bygones for them
Give them life, don't leave them forlorn.

88. Tears

Shed tears of sadness when you feel lost and deserted
Shed tears of happiness when your dreams are fulfilled,
Shed tears of victory when you have achieved your goal
Shed tears of generosity to your loved ones.

Shed tears of patience to handle a situation
Shed tears of anger when you lose faith,
Shed tears of craving when you are famished
Shed tears of magic when the Lord blesses your soul.

89. Hands

Use your hands to create a world of equality
Use your hands to help the sick and diseased,

Use your hands to make room for the downtrodden
Use your hands to spread a word of literacy,

Use your hands to love and bless the orphans
Use your hands to feed the thirsty and hungry,

Use your hands to lighten a candle at the altar
Use your hands to bathe your Lord with pure water,

Use your hands to fight for your nation
Use your hands to pray and do meditation.

90. Tides

The thunderous, roaring, blue tides of the sea
The high and the low with a vigorous flow,
Bring with them a sign of destruction and victory
Unstoppable, mysterious with a touch of laughter.

These tumultuous tides are full of anger
The endless and unfathomable sea,
Not a single soul will survive if they plunder
They visit the Earth, and carrying away the sin and sinner.

91. Knowledge

Let each one of us drink the cup of knowledge
Sip by sip, enjoy it up to the very last drop.

The scholars are continuously telling the layman
That future can only be secure if we learn to the core.

Forget not the strenuous writers of the past
They have laid their foundation till last.

They fathomed life and gave statements appropriate
Thousands have given a valuable message.

They can play with the words and sentences
They have brought out the vitality of the language.

Create an area for them and give a fresh start
They will always remain the leaders of the past.

92. Treasure

We treasure so many things, valuable in our life so dear

We hide them and keep them safe from eyes, full of fear.

They are close to our heart and we live our lives for them

The blatant truth is that they will pass on to somebody near.

Do not be attached, it is better to be detached

You will exit the world in the same way you entered.

So realise you have a temporary place on earth

Otherwise, these treasures will take away your mirth.

93. Books

I live with you

I breathe you in,

I inhale your fragrance

I am in love with you.

My heart beats for you

You made my life,

You gave me a room

In this vast universe.

I was unknown, unheard

Abandoned, lifeless,

Suddenly on cloud nine

He handed me a book.

I have a purpose now

There is a reason now,

I give myself to you now

I will not part with you now.

Your pages I read

Your images I perceive,

Your language I absorb

You are just like God.

94. Gateway

The gate is open now
I am in the seventh heaven,
My fingers are trembling
My body goes numb.

I hold it somehow
I push the gate gently,
I enter with soft steps
The noise I hear.

 The crushing of the leaves
Under my feet,
A faint light with cool breeze
He comes and holds my hand.

I enter the Garden of Eden
It is my Gateway,
To a world of Knowledge
I won't look back anyhow.

95. Peace

The need of the day, hour and minute
Is peace as the world is in a conflict

The nations are building cordial relationships
There is no need of bombs and warships

The patience is completely out of place now
Teach the people to be more at ease now

Learn to be tender and resilient
Keep repulsion at a greater distance

Go for ideas which bring unity and integrity
Learn to spread love without any formality

Blend yourself on this planet with humanity
All of you belong to the the same community.

96. Relationships

We build beautiful relationships in this universe

Try to be humble to the ones who know it's worth

There may be many who are still living in dearth.

Take the road to meet those who lent a helping hand

Always admire those who made you a man

It doesn't matter either they be rich or poor.

All these connections will be lost the day we leave this Earth

Develop one strong relationship with the creator of this Earth.

97. Cup of Tea

Don't be anybody's and everybody's cup of tea
A content soul it is better to be.

All are equal and born with the same calibre
Some use less, some greater.

Build your own identity
It is not advisable to make a plea.

Be headstrong and a shield maiden
Live unruffled, don't be overburdened.

98. Kadamba Tree

On one dark moonlit night, I had a strange dream
My steps turned towards the streets of Vrindavan.

Not a single soul was there in sight that night
Only the forest, dazzling under the stars bright.

A huge Kadamba Tree stood in the middle

The colourful Gopi's were about to giggle.

Waiting for their Lord to appear with his flute

A flash of light and there he stood.

I walked up and joined them to and fro

I was astonished I was one of them.

I danced throughout the dark night

At sunrise, he was out of sight.

99. Destiny

I am in a dilemma

Destiny…. Destiny,

You are following meI am following you.

I am still stuck

I know that time will tell

The panic begins

Strange destinations.

I may reach a grassland or a no man's land

I may reach a peaceful or a bustling bank,

I may become impoverished or affluent

I may lose or gain my patience

I may become incompetent or powerful.

My thoughts never take rest

I try to look at the best,

I'm counting my days

I want to stay safe.

100. Reason

We may have a thousand reasons to live

We may have a thousand reasons to die

Did you ever take into notice?

Your birth on this planet was a mystery

You do everything possible for a living

You laugh, cry and have reasons to enjoy

You fight, loose and come out as a winner

Did you ever remember your creator?

This is the final reason as you are a blessing.

Dr Harmeet Kaur Bhalla